WHAT IS EVANGELICALISM?

WHAT

IS

EVANGELICALISM?

Joel R. Beeke

PUBLISHING WITH A MISSION

EP BOOKS
Faverdale North
Darlington, DL3 0PH, England

web: http://www.epbooks.org

e-mail: sales@epbooks.org

First published 2012

British Library Cataloguing in Publication Data available

ISBN-13: 978-0-85234-779-9
ISBN-10: 0-85234-779-0

Unless otherwise indicated, all Scripture quotations are from the Holy Bible, Authorized (King James) Version.

Printed and bound in the USA.

CONTENTS

It is mere cant to cry, 'We are evangelical; we are all evangelical,' and yet decline to say what evangelical means. If men are really evangelical, they delight to spread as glad tidings the truths from which they take the name

(Charles Spurgeon).[1]

WHAT IS AN EVANGELICAL?

In 1976 the magazine *Newsweek* ran a cover story entitled 'The Year of the Evangelicals', a clear indication that by the mid-1970s evangelical Christianity[2] had attained public prominence in American media and politics. But about the same time, a poll of Americans who considered themselves to be evangelicals indicated that fifty per cent of them could not name even half of the Ten Commandments.[3]

What then is an evangelical? Different definitions are given depending on whom you ask. In this book we will (1) examine certain prevalent contemporary definitions; (2) develop a definition that is biblical, historical, confessional and practical; and (3) explore what it means to experience evangelicalism.

A variety of answers

In the sixteenth century Martin Luther spoke of the Protestant church as the Evangelical Church. The German adjective *evangelisch* means 'evangelical, Protestant, Lutheran'.[4] In many places in Europe and Russia today, 'evangelical' refers to any Christian who is not Roman Catholic or Eastern Orthodox. According to the Institute for the Study of American Evangelicals (ISAE), 'evangelical' is defined three ways. First, 'evangelical' refers to Christians who affirm certain doctrines and practices. Historian David Bebbington thus identifies four evangelical doctrines:

- *Biblicism*: the Bible is the only authoritative spiritual guide;
- *Crucicentrism*: Christ's death on the cross is the heart of faith and life;
- *Conversionism*: repentance from sin and faith in Christ are essential to salvation;

- *Activism*: Christians must work together to spread the gospel to all nations.[5]

John Stackhouse Jr, of the Evangelical Fellowship of Canada, adds the following two criteria to Bebbington's list of evangelical characteristics:

- *Orthodoxy/Orthopraxis*: Evangelicals subscribe to historic Christian doctrinal, ethical and liturgical tenets and practices;
- *Transdenominational*: Evangelicals partner with members of other churches in evangelistic, missionary, social and political activities.[6]

Second, according to the ISAE, 'evangelical' can also refer to a number of movements united as much by style as by belief or doctrine, and as such embraces a wide spectrum of people from Reformed to Pentecostal to Roman Catholic. Third, 'evangelical' can be used to describe certain publications or coalitions of men and institutions — such as the magazine *Christianity Today* and the Billy Graham Evangelistic Association — which sought a different path from the strident militancy and separatism of fundamentalism.[7]

Richard Lovelace says that 'the evangelical impulse' is 'an urgent drive to proclaim the saving, unmerited grace of Christ and to reform the church according to the Scriptures'.[8] In this he draws upon what are sometimes called the formal and material principles of the Reformation: the authority of Scripture alone, and salvation by faith in Christ alone.[9]

Yet another definition of 'evangelical' is provided by the 1846 constitution of the Evangelical Alliance, which adopted the following articles of faith: the divine inspiration of Scripture, the Trinity of persons in the Godhead, the depravity of man, the mediation of the divine Christ, justification by faith, conversion and sanctification by the Holy Spirit, the return of Christ to judge the world, the ministry of the Word, and the sacraments of baptism and the Lord's Supper.[10]

According to David Wells, people in the twentieth century viewed the core of evangelicalism in three ways. Some defined it as 'confessional', that is, its centre is the confession of specific biblical doctrines. Some saw evangelicalism as an 'organizational fraternity', a broad coalition of churches, missions, ministries, media and businesses, loosely united for various common causes or joint enterprises. Still others saw its core as 'charismatic', not in doctrine or organization, but in its 'spiritual intuition about the presence of the Holy Spirit'. The organizational and charismatic understandings of evangelicalism have taken the lead since the 1960s and 1970s, while the emphasis on the confessional definition has been relegated to the backseat.[11]

In answer to the question, 'What is an Evangelical?' the National Association of Evangelicals (NAE) in the United States states: 'Evangelicals take the Bible seriously and believe in Jesus Christ as Saviour and Lord.'[12] The NAE affirms a number of fundamental doctrines, but notably absent from this list is the doctrine of justification by faith alone.[13]

David Hilborn of the Evangelical Alliance in the United Kingdom says evangelicals are '"gospel people", committed to simple New Testament Christianity and the central tenets of apostolic faith', who are unified by the Reformation principles of Scripture alone, grace alone, and faith alone.[14]

Then, there are some who say we have no right to define evangelicalism or set any boundaries for it. Roger E. Olson says evangelicalism is a movement, not an organization, and therefore does not have defined boundaries, only 'certain common characteristics or family resemblances'. As a religious movement, evangelicalism cannot be precisely defined, and the identity of an evangelical likewise lacks any sort of precision. Anyone who tries to exclude another from the big tent of evangelicalism is acting the part of a bully, he says. Olson sees evangelical truth as 'a never-ending journey rather than a fortress to be defended'.[15] And yet, he also says that evangelicalism has a 'historical-theological core' of Christian orthodoxy, so long as no one requires 'slavish adherence' to its doctrines.[16] It has a centre, but no real boundaries; and even the centre is none too firmly fixed.

Meanwhile, polls seem to indicate that self-proclaimed evangelicalism in the United States is disintegrating in doctrinal and moral confusion. It is disheartening to hear the press's hyped-up and foolish statements against evangelicalism; news organizations and popular entertainment (television and cinema) focus on the extremists, hypocrites, and anything scandalous or sensational, such as the Florida pastor who made headlines all over the USA by threatening to burn, and then burning, a copy of the Koran.

James Boice defended evangelicalism, but had this to say, 'What is wrong with evangelicals? The answer is that we have become worldly. We have abandoned the truth of the Bible and the historic theology of the church, which expresses those truths, and we are trying to do the work of God by means of the world's "theology", wisdom, methods, and agenda instead.'[17] Boice said this was often less of a public renunciation of biblical truth as much as tragic neglect.

He wrote:

Does that mean that evangelicals deny the Bible or have officially turned their backs on classic Christian doctrine? Not necessarily. It is more often the case that the Bible's theology just does not have meaningful bearing on what we think or do… It has a lot to do with self-esteem, good mental attitudes, and worldly success. There is not much preaching about sin, hell, judgment, or the wrath of God, not to mention the great doctrines of the cross such as redemption, atonement, reconciliation, propitiation, justification, grace, and even faith.[18]

Due to confusion over the words 'evangelical' and 'evangelicalism' — evident in the various perspectives cited above — some Christians, including some Reformed Christians, have chosen to drop these terms altogether. D. G. Hart argues, for example, that believers may be 'better off if they relinquished the label [of "evangelical"] and academics might produce better scholarship on American religion if they ceased relying ironically on categories supplied by the owners of the evangelical construction company.'[19] As a movement, evangelicalism has become so unravelled and, as a confessional position, lost so much of its content, that in Hart's estimation the terminology no longer possesses meaning.

I believe that while much of what bears the name evangelical is shallow and even contrary to Scripture, the label itself is worth defending; I do not deny, however, that the term is a slippery fish to catch. To begin with, we must realize that evangelicalism needs both a firm centre and clearly delineated boundaries. If evangelicalism has no boundaries, then it has no meaning. R. Albert Mohler Jr has rightly noted: 'A word that can mean anything means nothing. If "evangelical identity" means drawing no boundaries, then we really have no centre, no matter what we may claim.'[20] If we say, for example, that Washington DC is the political centre of the United States but put no boundaries on its citizens, someone in Canada, Nigeria, or France could conceivably claim US citizenship simply because he has a T-shirt purchased in Washington DC!

Dr D. Martyn Lloyd-Jones said that in defining evangelicalism we face a twofold danger: our definition can be too narrow and thus be divisive and schismatic, or it can fall into blind ecumenicalism with the pretence that doctrine is unimportant as long as we all share the same Christian 'spirit' — whatever that may be.[21] Lloyd-Jones added some perceptive principles to guide our definition: (1) our goal must be the preservation of the gospel of salvation; (2) our attention must not merely focus on contemporary issues but also account for the history of the church; (3) we must ask not only what an organization stands for, but also what it stands against; (4) we must apply the definition not only by asking whether someone's statements agree with it, but also whether they neglect part of it, or add to it in a way that overthrows it.[22]

Having surveyed a variety of definitions of evangelicalism, let us now proceed to develop our own working definition.

DEFINING EVANGELICALISM

Our definition of evangelicalism must be biblical, historical, confessional and practical. We should consider these four areas to develop a true and integrated definition of what it means to be evangelical. Only after assessing each of these attributes in turn can we then present a concise and meaningful definition of evangelicalism.

The biblical roots of evangelicalism

The root meaning of the word 'evangelical' comes from the Greek word *euangelion*, which means 'good news' and is often translated 'gospel' in the New Testament. Although the word 'evangelical' does not appear in the Scriptures, its root meaning is 'of or pertaining to the gospel' or 'according to the gospel'. Thus our definition must be biblical, that is, it must accord with Scripture for the gospel is the central message of the Bible.

An evangelical Christian, then, is a Christian whose faith and life are determined by the biblical gospel. Truly evangelical people know the gospel, love the gospel, proclaim the gospel, and defend the gospel. So we should not be ashamed of being evangelicals any more than we should be ashamed of the gospel. Paul says in Romans 1:16, 'For I am not ashamed of the gospel of Christ: for it is the power of God unto salvation to every one that believeth; to the Jew first, and also to the Greek.'

Our definition of evangelical must therefore rest upon a biblical understanding of the gospel of Jesus Christ. The Scriptures portray the gospel as simple in its core, yet deep and rich in its fulness. We see the simplicity of the gospel in 1 Corinthians 15:1-5:

Moreover, brethren, I declare unto you the gospel which I preached unto you, which also ye have received, and wherein ye stand; by which also ye are saved, if ye keep in memory what I preached unto you, unless ye have believed in vain. For I delivered unto you first of all that which I also received, how that Christ died for our sins according to the scriptures; and that he was buried, and that he rose again the third day according to the scriptures: and that he was seen of Cephas, then of the twelve.

Paul here highlights seven central truths of the gospel:

1. It is an *authoritative message* from God: 'for I delivered unto you first of all that which I also received'. First Corinthians 11:23 says, 'For I have received of the Lord that which also I delivered unto you.' The gospel is God's message and it is not to be rejected or changed, but received and transmitted to others.

2. It presents the *unique person and mission* of Jesus Christ: Paul called Jesus the 'Christ' or the anointed one of God, alluding to the Old Testament anointing of prophets, priests and kings to mediate God's grace to his people. Jesus Christ is God's unique Son sent to save sinners.

3. It proclaims the *atoning death* of Christ: 'Christ died for our sins.' This means that Christ, the innocent One, received the punishment which we, due to our sin, deserved. He alone has atoned for the sins of his people. Neither our works nor our prayers can atone for sin.

4. It likewise proclaims the *bodily resurrection* of Christ: 'that he rose again the third day'. The resurrection confirms the validity of Christ's death as an atoning sacrifice, and secures our justification (Rom. 4:25). Likewise, Christ's resurrection fulfils his own prophecy (John 2:18-

22) and attests of his trustworthiness as a guide to salvation, and his identity as the incarnate Son of God.

5. It asserts the *historical reality* of these events: 'Christ died for our sins ... he was buried, and ... he rose again the third day ... and he was seen of Cephas, then of the twelve.' These are historical facts, the facts that constitute the foundation of the Christian faith; hence the prominence given to these facts in documents such as the *Apostles' Creed*. Paul's argument is that if these facts are not true, 'then is our preaching vain, and your faith is also vain' (v. 14), that is, meaningless, powerless and worthless.

6. It teaches the *sovereignty of God* over human history: twice Paul asserts that these things took place 'according to the scriptures'. Though Christ's death was carried out by human beings acting of their own will, God sovereignly directed everything they did in order to fulfil the promises recorded in the Old Testament (Acts 2:22-32).

7. It teaches the *necessity of faith in the biblical gospel*: 'the gospel which I preached unto you, which also ye have received, and wherein ye stand; by which also ye are saved'. This message is not an announcement that we are saved, but the preaching of Christ as Saviour, and the call to trust in him to be saved (Acts 16:31).

The gospel is fundamental to Christianity. All biblical doctrine is important and shapes our spiritual lives, but not all doctrine is fundamental, that is, foundational. The image of the foundation is found in 1 Corinthians 3, where Paul describes his ministry of the Word as laying the foundation 'which is Jesus Christ' (v. 11; see also Eph. 2:20), and other men as building on this foundation. Great theologians such as John Calvin and Francis Turretin recognized long ago that not all doctrine is fundamental to faith. A person can be a Christian and yet err in certain doctrines.[23] Calvin warned against dividing the church over secondary matters that do not overthrow the foundation:

> *For not all the articles of true doctrine are of the same sort. Some are so necessary to know that they should be certain and unquestioned by all men as the proper principles of religion. Such are: God is one; Christ is God and the Son of God; our salvation rests on God's mercy; and the like. Among the churches there are other articles of doctrine disputed which still do not break the unity of faith… Since all men are somewhat beclouded with ignorance, either we must leave no church remaining, or we must condone delusion in those matters which can go unknown without harm to the sum of religion and without loss of salvation.*[24]

The Bible also indicates that the gospel, for all its clarity and simplicity, is deeply profound and full of implications for the faith and life of God's people. It is a river from whose edge a lamb may safely drink and in whose middle an elephant may swim. Mark 1:1 introduces itself: 'The beginning of the gospel of Jesus Christ, the Son of God', meaning that his entire book is gospel. In Ephesians 3:6-7 Paul writes that God appointed him as a minister of 'the gospel', which in verse 8 he identifies as 'the unsearchable riches of Christ'. There is an infinite fulness to 'the gospel of the grace of God', which reveals to us 'all the counsel of God' (Acts 20:24, 27), 'which God Himself first revealed in Paradise; and afterwards published by the patriarchs and prophets, and represented by the sacrifices and other ceremonies of the law; and lastly, has fulfilled ... by His only begotten Son'.[25]

In 1999 a group of evangelicals, including Reformed and Arminian theologians, attempted to summarize the gospel. This effort, entitled 'The Gospel of Jesus Christ: An Evangelical Celebration', states: 'As evangelicals who derive our very name from the Gospel, we celebrate this great good news of God's saving work in Jesus Christ as the true bond of Christian unity.'[26] It is surprising that theologians from such different traditions could write a common statement of the gospel that was several pages long and included eighteen detailed affirmations and denials.

The gospel is like a well: at ground level we see a small, clearly-defined opening, but as we look deeper, a great depth is revealed. And as we draw from this well, we discover an infinite supply of truth and grace. The gospel in the deepest sense is Christ himself. The source of true evangelicalism, therefore, is found in the gospel as recorded in Scripture.

The history and heritage of evangelicalism

We live in a day when history and heritage are undervalued, even scorned. Sadly this is the case even among professing Christians. The term 'evangelical', however, is profoundly historical and must be treated as such. Richard Lovelace writes: 'Research into the historical roots of evangelicalism is one of the most fruitful and illuminating methods of resolving the identity crisis of the movement.' He argues that tracing our heritage back to its theological foundations in the sixteenth and seventeenth centuries brings 'a strong infusion of content into the evangelical label'.[27]

When we survey the history of Christianity, we see the church as the body of Christ. We read in

1 Corinthians 12:12: 'For as the body is one, and hath many members, and all the members of that one body, being many, are one body: so also is Christ.' Our union with Christ by faith in the gospel unites us with all believers, not just in this age, but throughout the ages. The contemporary church is organically joined to the historic church; we are thus surrounded by a great cloud of witnesses from Abel to Augustine and from Moses to John Murray.

If the root of the evangelical tree is the biblical gospel, arguably its historical trunk is the Protestant Reformation. While the term 'evangelical' is rooted in Scripture, it did not come into common usage until the sixteenth century, when Martin Luther and other Reformers labelled themselves evangelicals in contrast to the Roman Catholic Church.[28] They were not hereby claiming there were no gospel believers in the Roman church, nor did they believe that the gospel was not preached prior to their own time; they did believe, however, that many human traditions had obscured the gospel and that during the Reformation the gospel shone forth with greater clarity, brilliance and soul-igniting heat.

Today, however, it is common to define evangelicalism in terms of the eighteenth-century revivals in the English-speaking world.[29] There is some truth to this. The Great Awakening profoundly shaped evangelicalism in Britain and America. But

I believe it is best to understand evangelicalism as a movement that began in the sixteenth-century Protestant Reformation, for Luther and Calvin considered themselves to be teachers of the evangelical faith.[30] Out of the Reformation sprang the Puritan movement that flourished in the late sixteenth and early seventeenth centuries. The Puritans often used the term *evangelical* to describe faith and obedience rooted in the gospel. Leaders involved in the eighteenth-century revivals, such as Jonathan Edwards and George Whitefield, saw themselves as the descendants and heirs of both the Reformers and the Puritans.[31]

The nineteenth century is often regarded as the great age of evangelicalism, in terms of church growth, evangelism, missions, colleges and seminaries, and even political influence and social reform. All of this was eclipsed in the early twentieth century with the rise of fundamentalism. As evangelicalism developed in the mid-twentieth century, its progenitors believed that they were simply preserving and propagating 'Protestant orthodoxy' and 'mainstream Christianity', not a sectarian 'ism'.[32] Vernon Grounds said of the American Evangelical movement in 1956: 'This, then, is the nature of Protestant orthodoxy, a twentieth century continuation of the historic faith which springs from a bloody cross and an empty tomb, a protest against religious deviants from the

Gospel of redemption, a witness to the truth and grace of God in Jesus Christ.'[33]

We must also recognize that evangelicalism is a global phenomenon. While many historians and social scientists limit their study of evangelicalism to Britain or North America, the largest numbers of evangelicals today are found in Africa and Asia. We do our brothers in Korea, China, Nigeria, South Africa, and other nations a disservice if we omit them from the evangelical picture. This is another reason to establish the historical basis of evangelicalism in the Protestant Reformation, for the Reformation has always been a multi-national movement. It began in Germany but spread to France, Switzerland, Scotland, England, Hungary, Poland, the Netherlands, Sweden, Norway, Finland and Iceland, and eventually to the New World.

So while recognizing the distinctive origin and progress of evangelicalism in different nations and ages, we should see it historically as a continuous movement that first expressed itself in the Reformation, then flowed forward through Puritanism and Pietism into the First and Second Great Awakenings and to all the world through missions and the founding of indigenous churches.

This history means we cannot define evangelicalism as something within the limits of the Reformed faith. It would be historically inaccurate to say that only Reformed Christians are evangelical. We must recognize that Lutherans also are part of the evangelical movement. To be Reformed is a subset of being evangelical, a circle that is, for the most part, within a larger circle. That is to say, ideally speaking, evangelicalism is primarily *Reformation* Christianity, though at times the history of evangelicalism seems to be nearly as much a history of dissent from the Reformation as a history of affirmation of Reformation truth.

To mention only a few examples, John Wesley represented a significant movement in the Church of England to modify Calvinism in the way proposed in the Netherlands by James Arminius. Then we have the Anabaptists and the Pietists who influenced Wesley, the Mennonities, the Herrnhutters, and the Moravians. If the English Baptists were originally Calvinistic, later generations of England and North America in the late nineteenth and early twentieth centuries cast off Calvinism in favour of Arminianism and never looked back. As for the original evangelicals, today as always a large party in the Church of England, they also represent a theological spectrum ranging from Calvinistic (think J. I. Packer) to Arminianism, to doctrinal indifference or else theological eclecticism (think John Stott). Yet all these and many more have long had a seat at the evangelical table — in fact, for every Calvinistic evangelical today, there may be scores of Arminian evangelicals. I do not mean to say that all Anabaptists, Anglicans, Wesleyan Methodists, Pentecostals and Charismatics, and others who reject some substantial Reformation doctrines to varying degrees, are to be regarded as evangelicals, for then the term *evangelical* would indeed be 'watery', amorphous and meaningless, but there certainly are some in all of these groups who would adhere to a basically sound definition of the gospel and its application, who can justly be called evangelicals despite rejecting certain areas of Reformation doctrine.

The idea that a person can be an evangelical Roman Catholic, however, is self-contradictory, for the Roman church rejected the core of the evangelical doctrines of the Reformers at the Council of Trent. Either a person is faithful to the basics of the gospel defined by the Reformation, or he is faithful to the teachings of Rome about salvation. Nor is it enough for a person or organization to reject Roman Catholicism to be considered an evangelical, for evangelicalism that largely abandons its Reformation heritage is not evangelical at all.

Despite all this, the historical trunk of evangelicalism implies that our definition should be guided by the theological guidelines of the Reformers.

Often this common Reformation heritage is identified by the five *solas* that guard the gospel:[34]

1. *Sola Scriptura*: Scripture alone, not human tradition and reasoning, determines our faith and commands our obedience. This means that evangelicals are suspicious of fallen reason and always want to test their beliefs and practices by the Holy Scriptures.We receive the Scriptures 'not as the word of men, but as it is in truth, the word of God' (1 Thess. 2:13), truthful, authoritative and without error. So evangelicals reject attempts to subject the Bible to the judgement of finite human reasoning. Our minds are servants to receive the Word, not to judge it. The church does not construct the truth but draws it from Scripture by faithful exposition, reflection and application. If God is God, then he is beyond our comprehension and his Word holds absolute authority. It also means that we reject anyone who claims to be an infallible prophet for God today.[35]

2. *Sola Gratia*: Grace alone, not human goodness and effort, saves sinners. Evangelical Christians do not look for salvation in their baptism, their good works, or taking part at the Lord's Table. They do not (or should not) trust their methods

or will-power. Salvation belongs to the Lord. We resonate with the words of Christ: 'Ye must be born again' (John 3:7). This implies that mankind is deeply corrupted by sin and we are unable to save ourselves.

3. *Solus Christus*: Christ alone, not the saints or the ministry and rites of the church, stands as our Mediator and our Deliverer. 'For there is one God, and one mediator between God and men, the man Christ Jesus' (1 Tim. 2:5). We live by faith in the Son of God, who loved us and gave himself for us (Gal. 2:20). No angel, no man, no heavenly spirit — only Jesus Christ can be our Prophet, Priest and King. Christ is not merely the door into the kingdom; he is the entire way we must travel to glory. 'And ye are complete in him' (Col. 2:10). Christ is 'unto us wisdom, and righteousness, and sanctification, and redemption' (1 Cor. 1:30).

4. *Sola Fide*: Faith alone, not our works, is the instrument by which the sinner receives and rests upon Christ and his righteousness, and is justified from the guilt of all sin (Gal. 2:16). Evangelical Christians are deeply concerned with how a sinner can be right with God. They are convinced that no amount of sincerity, love, good deeds, or

acts of devotion can atone for our sins and make us righteous before God. 'Now to him that worketh is the reward not reckoned of grace, but of debt. But to him that worketh not, but believeth on him that justifieth the ungodly, his faith is counted for righteousness' (Rom. 4:4-5). We must simply trust, receiving Christ as with the empty hand of a beggar. We have no merit in ourselves.

5. *Soli Deo Gloria*: Our salvation is attributed to God alone, 'to the praise of His glorious grace'. Ideally, evangelical Christianity honours our leaders, but does not elevate them to a higher level than other sinners saved by grace. Our worship is reserved for God (Rev. 19:10). Therefore evangelicalism rejects all prayer or devotion to the saints, and the worship of any god except the triune God of the Bible. We also reject taking any credit for our own salvation or good works, but know that all the glory for any good to us, in us, or through us must be given to God through Jesus Christ (1 Cor. 4:7; Gal. 6:14).

The Alliance of Confessing Evangelicals rightly takes its stand on these five *solas* of the Reformation as set forth in the *Cambridge Declaration* of 1996.[36]

Reformation truths have always been the heart of evangelicalism. Martin Luther said in his *Large*

Catechism,' ... God does not lie. My neighbor and I —
in short, all people — may deceive and mislead, but
God's Word cannot deceive.'[37] These truths shaped
the preaching of such diverse figures as Jonathan
Edwards and John Wesley in the eighteenth century,
Charles Spurgeon and Dwight L. Moody in the
nineteenth century, and D. Martyn Lloyd-Jones and
A. W. Tozer in the twentieth century. Wesley said, 'I
receive the written word as the whole and sole rule
of my faith.'[38] Wesley also said,

> *God himself has condescended to teach the way; for
> this very end he came from heaven. He hath written
> it down in a book. O give me that book! At any
> price give me the book of God! I have it: here is
> knowledge enough for me. Let me be* Homo unius
> libri *[a man of one book].*[39]

I am not saying all these men were Reformed.
Wesley certainly was not, but the Reformation
solas profoundly shaped his doctrine and life as an
evangelical.

We also need to recognize that the Reformation
legacy includes much wisdom from the patristic and
medieval church. The gospel root was not dead for
fifteen hundred years prior to the Reformation. If
you cut into the trunk of a large tree, you see dozens
of rings representing years of development. So also

the Reformers, and the Puritans after them, drew a wealth of doctrine from the wisdom of the Church Fathers, especially the doctrines of God, the Trinity, and the incarnation of Christ. The Reformers found in the Augustinian tradition a breathtaking vision of the beauty of the triune God and the potential for soul-satisfying communion with him. They and the Puritans regularly quoted such men as Augustine and Bernard of Clairvaux in gathering the gold of historic Christianity, purified by the Word.

The root of evangelicalism is found in the biblical gospel. The trunk of this beautiful tree is the historic church, preeminently seen in the Reformation.

The confessional branches of evangelicalism

The *Cambridge Declaration* of the Alliance of Confessing Evangelicals says, 'Historic evangelicalism was confessional.'[40] So our definition of evangelicalism must have a confessional dimension. By confession I mean the church's historic creeds and summations of her doctrine and standards for the life of her members. The church's confession of faith springs first from the gospel. The Lord Jesus Christ said that we must confess him before men if we want him to confess us on Judgement Day (Matt. 10:32). Paul writes that confessing our faith in Christ is a fundamental part of a saving faith in Jesus Christ (Rom. 10:9-10). The church of the living God is 'the pillar and ground of the truth', one which publicly confesses and defends 'the mystery of god-liness' (1 Tim. 3:15-16).

Our definition of evangelicalism must be confessional because it must grow out of 'the unity of the faith' (Eph. 4:13). This may be very unpopular today, since doctrine is often seen as divisive, and agreement in doctrine unnecessary, but it is impossible to define evangelicalism without referring to certain articles of faith. Indeed we have a God-given duty to do so, for Jude 3 says, 'Beloved, when I gave all diligence to write unto you of the common salvation, it was needful for me to write unto you, and exhort you that ye should earnestly contend for the faith which was once delivered unto the saints.'

In 2008 a group of Christians published *An Evangelical Manifesto*, which contained this statement: 'Evangelicals adhere fully to the Christian faith expressed in the historic creeds of the great ecumenical councils of the church, and in the great affirmations of the Protestant Reformation.'[41] It also states: 'Evangelicalism must be defined theologically and not politically; confessionally and not culturally.'[42]

Joseph Stowell writes:

Evangelicals, then, are a family united in the Gospel of Jesus Christ. We come from many nations, races, economic circumstances, denominations, and churches. The geographic boundaries for the family are as large as the world itself. But the doctrinal boundaries are circumscribed by a commitment to the Gospel of Jesus Christ … in particular and to the historic tenets of orthodox Christian truth in general, as described in the Holy Scriptures.[43]

Similarly, Albert Mohler writes:

Though evangelicalism has never been reducible to theological conviction alone, it cannot remain evangelical and be satisfied with anything less than theological fidelity.[44]

If evangelicalism is to be defined confessionally, then what must its confession of faith be? We cannot choose a Reformed confession of faith for this would automatically exclude all non-Reformed. I use the image of branches on a tree to suggest that evangelicalism is not defined by a single confession but a large number of confessions growing out of the same tree. History makes that plain, for the trunk of Reformation Christianity quickly developed branches. In Germany grew the Lutheran and German Reformed branches; in France and

Switzerland, the French Reformed branch; in the Netherlands, the Dutch Reformed Evangelical branch; in Scotland, the Presbyterian branch; and in England, the Anglican branch. Out of the Anglican branch sprouted the Puritan branch, and out of the Puritan branch came the Congregationalist and Baptist branches. And still later, the Methodist branch emerged from Anglicanism, and from Methodism various types of holiness groups. All of these branches were evangelical because they all sprang from the Reformation. Each branch in turn produced distinct confessions of faith, but all confessed the same biblical gospel.

This image of many branches from one tree also has implications for our definition. The Lutheran churches do not adhere to the same doctrines of predestination and calling that the Reformed churches do. Neither do the Wesleyan Methodists. We Reformed Christians believe that these brothers undermine the principle of *sola gratia* or 'grace alone'. These brethren disagree with us, but we cannot exclude each other from being evangelicals without being historically inaccurate. As we have already stated, evangelicalism is not the same thing as Reformed Christianity; it is a broader category than that. Thus evangelicalism must be defined to reflect the unity and diversity present in the Reformation and its later developments in history.

This is not to paper over the Calvinist/Arminian difference among evangelicals. Generally speaking, I think B. B. Warfield has the answer for this thorny problem. The Wesleyans were guilty of living with an inherent contradiction. They wanted to affirm that 'salvation is of the Lord' and that the choice or decision lies with man as a free agent. So they were, in Warfield's term, 'inconsistent evangelicals', where Calvinism is 'consistent evangelicalism'.[45]

Nor am I suggesting that every organization historically linked to a Reformation church is evangelical. It is evangelical only if it remains faithful to the riches of Christ found in the gospel. At some point infidelity kills a branch, and it ultimately falls to the ground. Thus we can rightfully challenge liberal Protestant churches, asking: 'Are you faithful to your own confessions? If not, have you reformed your churches by Scripture alone, or are you drifting from your gospel roots?' Sadly, every branch of evangelical Christianity will die if it is not vigilant for the truth of God. We need to cherish our Reformation confessions as faithful declarations of biblical, historic Christianity, to keep us anchored in evangelical truth and faith.

Some organizations use a minimal statement of faith to identify themselves as evangelical. They have a lowest-common-denominator confession, consisting of a handful of doctrinal points or emphases. They want to stick to the fundamentals, but defining evangelicalism by a bare-bones statement of faith creates serious problems.

First, we are not talking here about the fundamental doctrines a person must believe to be saved, but the doctrines that define a Christian movement. If a church is to be considered evangelical, its pastors and elders must adhere to more than a minimalist gospel. Titus 1:9 defines an elder as someone 'holding fast the faithful word as he hath been taught, that he may be able by sound doctrine both to exhort and to convince the gainsayers'.

Second, if we try to define evangelicalism with a short list of fundamentals, our list will have gaping holes. Short statements of faith assume too much by failing to address certain foundational matters and thus leave open doors for soul-damning error, such as 'Open Theism', which says that God does not know (or care) what you will eat for lunch tomorrow.[46] Our brief statements of faith are powerless to address such issues because they say nothing about God's foreknowledge and sovereign decree. One must go back to the Christian orthodoxy expressed in the older Reformation confessions to deal with such issues.[47]

Third, minimal statements of faith have left evangelicalism doctrinally impoverished in certain areas, but in others — take eschatology, for example — obsessive compulsive. Consider ecclesiology, the doctrine of the church. We know that Presbyterians, Baptists and Lutherans disagree strongly about worship, the officers of the church, and church polity, so we cannot adopt one confession of faith in these matters. On the other hand, many evangelicals have adopted such a bland, generic position on worship that they have invited worldliness into the church. Albert Mohler writes: 'Given the cultural transformations and the absence of biblical knowledge and sustained theological reflection, many evangelicals seem to have virtually no ecclesiology at all.'[48] People who think the Bible has nothing definitive to say about the church's worship and order should ground themselves in the rich ecclesiology of the confessions of the sixteenth and seventeenth centuries. We must not sacrifice our church's confession on the altar of evangelical ecumenism. We need to hold on to the biblical substance of our distinctions, while showing respect for other evangelical people.

Fourth, minimal statements of faith result in a fragmented perspective of life which leaves the church open for the invasion of worldly mindsets. Biblical orthodoxy is a grand panorama of truth, stretching from creation to new creation, revealing the riches of the wisdom and knowledge of God.

Individual statements without the context of the biblical narrative lose their meaning and significance. They are but a handful of puzzle pieces without the whole of the puzzle. We need the big picture. Particular truths, however accurately stated, cannot replace a comprehensive God-centred view of truth. The Reformation confessions and catechisms express this view; they show us the big picture, the great panorama of truth.

Why do so many evangelical Christians today have so little knowledge of the Reformation confessions and Christian doctrine? Historically, they may have reacted against distortions of Reformation confessional Christianity. The Free Church movement on the continent, in Scandinavia and elsewhere, came out of Pietism's reaction to dead orthodoxy and persecuting state churches. The fundamentalist movement reacted against the unbelief of Protestant 'modernism', which, as J. Gresham Machen observed, was really not Christianity at all but another religion entirely.[49] The 'new evangelicals' reacted against the legalism and belligerence of fundamentalism and wanted to pursue a more thoughtful faith, a more winsome evangelism, and a more positive engagement as salt and light in the world. Now it seems people in the 'emergent churches' are reacting against the superficiality of the 'new evangelicals'.

To all persons who identify themselves as evangelical Christians, let me offer an invitation and a warning. I sympathize with your desire for a living, personal faith that is faithful to the Holy Scriptures, rooted in the past, separated from the world, and yet engaged in evangelism and works of mercy in the world. I invite you, therefore, to consider again the Reformation confessions. Start by reading the *Westminster Shorter Catechism* or the *Heidelberg Catechism*. You will find a vibrant personal faith; not oppression and tyranny, but Christian freedom; not divisive doctrine but, as Paul wrote in Ephesians 4:13, 'the unity of the faith, and of the knowledge of the Son of God'. These catechisms reflect not just the insights of the Reformation but the wisdom of the church throughout the ages. Read the Scripture references given with every answer and you will discover that this is the doctrine of God, not man. Even if you cannot in good conscience subscribe to these confessions in their entirety, read them, study them, use them, and find your evangelical identity in them. Do not cast aside the wealth of truth God gave to his church through teachers like Luther, Calvin, Ursinus, the Westminster Divines, and many others.

With this invitation I offer a warning. One reason why people have so little appreciation for detailed doctrinal statements like the Reformation confessions is that they no longer believe God's Word gives us clear and certain knowledge about what to believe and how to live. They think it is arrogant to have firm convictions about anything beyond a simple gospel presentation. This, dear friends, is not humility, but a scepticism and rejection of the clarity, authority and necessity of the Scriptures. If this type of thinking prevails, it will ruin evangelicalism and give way to feel-good relativism, agnosticism and atheism. Carl Trueman writes:

> *I was talking recently to the head of a parachurch organization who was telling me how disheartened he was at the lack of doctrinal understanding among many of the young people applying to him for work. They loved the Lord Jesus; but they seemed to know next to nothing about Him. This is very worrying, for ... such lack of doctrinal knowledge actually indicates a lack of a deep and meaningful relationship with Christ.*[50]

While we can summarize the gospel in a few simple truths (as we did earlier from 1 Corinthians 15), this gospel core depends upon a broader system of biblical truths reflected in the larger, richer, fuller confessions of faith. Our definition of evangelicalism must make reference to all branches of the tree, represented by the family of confessions springing from the Reformation.

The practical fruits of evangelicalism

Christ said that we know a tree by its fruits
(Matt. 7:16). This is also true of our metaphor of
evangelicalism as a tree rooted in the gospel of Jesus
Christ. The gospel is fruitful, productive, powerful,
mighty to save, and able to change lives. Thus to be
true evangelical Christians, we need more than a
dead repetition of orthodox doctrines. We need a
lively orthodoxy that produces orthopraxy, that is,
'right faith' that results in 'right practice', a living
faith seen by its works (James 2:26).

It is possible for a person to be an active member
of a Reformed confessional church and yet not
be evangelical. Of course, they might be rebelling
against their own confession, but failing to be
evangelical can be much more subtle. David Wells
writes of 'the emptying out of the inner life of
evangelicalism', saying, '[t]heological ideas, rather
than being rejected, simply lose their power to
shape evangelical life'.[51] People pay lip service to
their confession, but their hearts are not ruled by
biblical truth. They are ruled by the world and its
deceptions. So our definition of evangelicalism must
be more than confessional; it must also be practical.

We cannot define evangelicalism by right practice
in every detail of life. The movement then would
be very small indeed, for only Christ obeyed God

perfectly. The rest of us are confused and disobedient and distorted images of God at best. How, then, can we identify evangelicalism by its practical fruit without becoming legalists or perfectionists? Again let us turn to the biblical, historical and confessional dimensions of evangelicalism.

The biblical dimension tells us that evangelical Christians are people of the gospel. Evangelicalism echoes the words of Acts 20:21: 'testifying both to the Jews, and also to the Greeks, repentance toward God, and faith toward our Lord Jesus Christ'. Simply put, evangelical Christians receive the gospel gladly, and tell others about it.

This gospel also produces a life which is fitting or worthy of the gospel. One thinks of Paul's command in Philippians 1:27: 'Only let your conversation [i.e. your manner of life] be as it becometh the gospel of Christ.' Paul further tells us in his epistle that this life is one of:

- standing and striving as a team for the mission of the gospel (Ch. 1);
- humility, serving others, and obeying God through self-sacrifice (Ch. 2);
- despising our self-righteousness to pursue Christ as our great desire (Ch. 3);
- rejoicing and contentment, and hope in the Lord (Ch. 4).

In a word, for the evangelical 'to live is Christ' (Phil. 1:21) — living in Christ, like Christ, by Christ, for Christ. If the gospel produces any fruit within us, it is in loving Jesus Christ and likeness to him.

The historical and confessional dimensions also help us here. When the Reformation churches wrote their confessions and catechisms, they turned again and again to two great sources of practical Christianity: the Ten Commandments and the Lord's Prayer. It is ludicrous for a church to claim to be evangelical if it rejects the basic morality taught by the church for centuries and advocates antinomianism or moral relativism. And yet, tragically, it often was self-confessed 'evangelical' Christians who led the way throughout the last century in discarding the Ten Commandments as a rule of life. It is also patently ridiculous for us to call ourselves evangelical if we are not a people of prayer, especially prayer for God's kingdom to come through the preaching of the gospel to all nations.

True evangelicalism is practical, for the gospel produces fruit.

Summary: a definition of evangelicalism

Having walked through the steps of what it means to be biblical, historical, confessional and practical, we are prepared to answer the question: What is evangelicalism? Let me offer a short definition, followed by a longer exposition. *Evangelicalism is gospel-driven Christianity, recognizable by the biblical fundamentals of the gospel of Christ, the Reformation fulness of the doctrines of Christ, and the practical fruit of the Spirit of Christ.* Now let me expound that more fully.

Evangelicalism is gospel-driven Christianity, recognizable by:

- The biblical fundamentals of the gospel of Christ, namely, the divine authority of Scripture; the deity and humanity of Jesus Christ as the incarnate Son of God; the atonement for sin by Christ's death; the gift of eternal life by Christ's resurrection; the historical reality of God's works of creation, providence and redemption; the sovereignty of God over history to fulfil his plan; and the necessity of faith in the mediatorial work of Jesus Christ for personal salvation.
- The Reformation fulness of the doctrines of Christ, that is, the wider context of biblical truth in which the gospel itself is rooted, distilled in the Reformation confessions and safeguarded by the Reformation watchwords of Scripture alone, grace alone, Christ alone, faith alone, and the glory of God alone.

- The practical fruit of the Spirit of Christ, including love for God, a passionate desire to know Jesus Christ, to live by faith in him, to obey the law of God, to serve others in love and humility, to prayerfully depend on God, to seek his glory in all things, and to unite in the support of missions, the spreading of the gospel.

Evangelicalism is a tree with many branches, but it also has organic unity. The tree of evangelicalism consists of the life-giving root of the gospel, the strong trunk of the Reformation, the various branches of the sixteenth and seventeenth-century confessions growing out of the Reformation, and the sweet and wholesome fruit of the practical life of Christ within us.

This definition raises some questions. We might ask: 'What is the relationship between evangelical Christianity and Roman Catholicism?' Here we need to distinguish between Roman Catholics and Roman Catholicism. The system of doctrine, liturgy and practice coming from Rome, which we call Roman Catholicism, is contradictory to much of evangelicalism's Reformation heritage (exceptions, of course, include Rome's affirmation of the Holy Trinity, the deity and humanity of Christ, the *Apostles' Creed*, etc.). We cannot say that evangelicalism and Roman Catholicism are two circles that nearly overlap. We long and pray for the Roman Catholic Church to repent of her errors and embrace the biblical *evangel* of justification by faith alone (not our baptism, penitence, or good works) and through the mediation of Christ alone (not Mary, the saints, or the church's priesthood). However, individual Roman Catholics may be gospel-believing Christians if they are ignorant of their church's doctrines or in rebellion against them. To such we say, 'Come out from among them and walk with us. Do you love the true gospel? Join the true evangelical church.'

Someone might ask: 'What is the relationship between evangelicalism and Pentecostalism?' That is a difficult question because historic Pentecostalism and the latter-day charismatic movement are complicated phenomena. They have set the modern agenda when it comes to evangelical worship, for example — or evangelical 'culture' as one can hear by listening to most 'Christian' radio stations. They boast of being a 'third force' in world Christianity, that is, neither Roman Catholic nor Protestant, but something other, something new in the world — all the while remaining vocally evangelical!

Some of these people claim that their leader speaks with infallible, divine authority. They have grossly violated the principle of Scripture alone, and set up a man as a little pope. Even more serious is the denial of the Trinity on the part of the 'oneness' wing of Pentecostalism. They are not true evangelicals. Others are more humble; they believe in continuing revelation but try to honour the supreme authority of the Bible. Such persons are still mistaken in not receiving the Scriptures as the fully sufficient Word, but I do not see all of them as outside of evangelicalism because of confusion on this point. I simply warn them not to let their emotions carry them away from sound doctrine and lead them to accept whatever seems to come with emotional fervour.

Another question that might arise is: 'What should we make of Bebbington's fourfold definition of evangelicalism that is commonly used today?' I think his definition, though insightful, is abused by some people. For example, evangelical 'biblicism' is more than a high regard for the Bible; we see the Bible as the only inerrant, verbally inspired, divinely authoritative, fully sufficient rule of faith and obedience. Evangelical 'crucicentrism' is more than a devotional attachment to the cross — which could express itself in the contemplation of a crucifix — but is the soul's resting upon God's written promise that his Son died as the substitute for sinners. He took their curse for them, and anyone who trusts in Christ alone is declared righteous by God without regard to man's works. Evangelical 'conversionism' is shaped by the doctrine of salvation by grace alone, resulting in a new birth and new creation worked by the Spirit of God through the gospel — not merely a reformation of outward behaviour or a new religious affiliation. The heartbeat of evangelical 'activism' is not merely social justice or church growth, as desirable as such things are. Evangelical mission work is fuelled by the fear of the One who casts into the fires of hell all who do not receive the gospel. It is energized by the joy of seeing God glorified by every nation in every neighbourhood of every place on earth.

Furthermore, Bebbington's definition of evangelicalism misses key ingredients of the evangelical identity. Consider but two essential characteristics overlooked in Bebbington's definition. First, the doctrine of God, the contemplation of his glorious attributes and triune personality, is the core of the evangelical's faith and devotion. Second, without the doctrine of human sin, with its heinous, wrath-provoking offence against God and its soul-ruining enslavement and pervasive depravity, the evangelical message of salvation makes no sense. It is quickly replaced with something more appealing to wicked men. Kenneth Kantzer wrote:

All would admit, for example, that the doctrine of the trinity is essential to historical Christianity and certainly also to evangelicalism. The divine attributes of omniscience, omnipotence, omnipresence, eternality, holiness, love, and truth are clearly fundamentals of any biblical Christian faith. No complete listing of evangelical faith could omit the doctrine of creation and divine providence; of man created in the image of God; of the fall, in which this image was thoroughly defaced but not completely eradicated; and of sin as inherited corruption and guilt.[52]

We need the fulness of doctrine as found in the Reformation confessions to provide the proper context in which we can see the true meaning and relevance of the fundamentals of the gospel. No short list of doctrines will do.

Some might also ask: 'What is the relationship between Reformed Christianity and evangelical Christianity?' I speak here, not of Reformed Christianity in its fatal distortions of hyper-Calvinism and dead orthodoxy, but in its true sense of biblical, Reformed, experiential, practical Christianity. I suggest that 'Reformed' is not the same thing as 'evangelical', but neither is it altogether separate. Reformed Christianity is the centre of ideal evangelical Christianity. In the history of the British Isles and America, again and again God has used the preaching of Reformed truth to renew and revive his people, in their love for the gospel, and desire to see it proclaimed to the ends of the earth.

If evangelicalism is really the broad effect of the reformation and revival of the church by the Holy Spirit, then we must do more than simply define it. We want to experience it. This leads to the final section of this book.

Experiencing evangelicalism

Robert Burns (1789–1869), in introducing Thomas Halyburton's *Works* (1674–1712), said that 'experimental' or experiential religion is 'Christianity brought home to "men's business and bosoms"'. He wrote: 'Christianity should not only be known, and understood, and believed, but also felt, and enjoyed, and practically applied.'[53] The Puritans who wrote the *Westminster Confession* said, 'A most sovereign antidote against all kinds of errors, is to be grounded and settled in the faith … But yet the knowledge we especially commend, is not a brain-knowledge, a mere speculation … but an inward, a savoury, an heart knowledge.'[54] By 'savoury' the Puritans meant tasting of and delighting in the spiritual realities revealed in Scripture (Ps. 34:8). This is true of Reformation Christianity, but, sadly, much of the heart of evangelicalism today has been seriously diluted due to the subtle influence of liberalism.

In 1937 Richard Niebuhr wrote this description of liberalism: 'A God without wrath brought men without sin into a kingdom without judgment through the ministrations of a Christ without a cross.'[55] Niebuhr was not an evangelical theologian. Nevertheless he saw clearly what most liberal theologians would not admit. The 'modernism' of the twentieth century consisted largely in the negation and rejection of historic Christian doctrines, with little or nothing to take their place. The result was that the sword of the Spirit was wrapped in a thousand layers of bland reassurances and empty slogans ('the brotherhood of man and the fatherhood of God') and quietly put in the attic. There was no gospel left to preach, only deadly silence. As Niebuhr put it, whereas Jonathan Edwards, for example, struggled to adjust himself to God's sovereignty, liberalism 'established continuity between God and man by adjusting God to man'.[56] Niebuhr's words pinpoint the problem of many of today's so-called 'evangelicals': the neglect or denial of God's sovereignty, human sin and depravity, and the uniqueness of Christ's death as the ransom for sinners.

What of value is then left to experience in evangelicalism? Much of what I am about to write on experiencing evangelicalism could be characterized by many as wishful thinking. As a friend recently wrote to me: 'I have experienced evangelicalism since I was a teenager, in many of its classic forms, in youth groups, the Graham crusades, charismatic meetings, parachurch campus ministries, even beach evangelism and televangelism (the PTL Club and Michigander Dutchman Jim Bakker). The threefold experience of grace posited in the *Catechism* (i.e., misery, deliverance, gratitude) was the exception, not the rule. Thanks to the influence of converted salesmen like Dwight L. Moody and Bill Bright of Campus Crusade, we had a much more efficient way to produce evangelical Christians, walking them through the Four Spiritual Laws from sin to salvation in a matter of minutes. Today, thanks to the televangelists, there doesn't have to be any content at all to faith, just a rush of feeling.'

My friend writes all too accurately. And yet, one can still aim for the ideal — that is, the experience of true evangelicalism in its biblical Reformation roots. To experience true, historic, experiential evangelicalism (yes, I'm aiming for the ideal here) is to experience the Word of God with its sharp edges stripping away our self-delusions and cutting deep into the soul. Hebrews 4:12 says, 'For the word of God is quick, and powerful, and sharper than any two-edged sword, piercing even to the dividing asunder of soul and spirit, and of the joints and marrow, and is a discerner of the thoughts and intents of the heart.'

Experiencing the heavenly majesty of God

Isaiah 66:1-2 says, 'Thus saith the LORD, The heaven is my throne, and the earth is my footstool: where is the house that ye build unto me? and where is the place of my rest? For all those things hath mine hand made, and all those things have been, saith the LORD: but to this man will I look, even to him that is poor and of a contrite spirit, and trembleth at my word.'

Nominal evangelicalism looks at the works of human hands and boasts about growing churches, schools and colleges, evangelistic crusades, television and radio ministries, publishing houses, and especially political clout. True experiential evangelicalism bows in humility before God. The vast heavens are the works of his fingers. The whole earth is a mere footstool for him. The nations are as dust in the scales, and a drop in the bucket. God needs nothing from us, and our whole duty before him can be summed up: 'Fear God, and keep his commandments' (Eccles. 12:13).

The great end of preaching is to communicate the glory of God in Jesus Christ. Lloyd-Jones said, 'I can forgive a man for a bad sermon, I can forgive the preacher almost anything if he gives me a sense of God ... some dim glimpse of the majesty and the glory of God.'[57] John Piper wrote of Charles

Spurgeon: 'There has scarcely been a pastor with more popular appeal. But his messages were full of God, and the atmosphere was charged with the presence of awesome realities.'[58] Cotton Mather said, 'The great design and intention of the office of a Christian preacher are to restore the throne and dominion of God in the souls of men.'[59] To fill the mind's eye with the infinite glory and holiness of the Lord so that the heart is shattered by the knowledge of one's sins, and the believer trembles in awe — this is experiential Christianity.

Experiencing the majesty of God is not just one department of Christian experience; it is the aim of the entire Christian life. God's law makes known his glory, for Isaiah 42:21 says, 'The LORD is well pleased for his righteousness' sake; he will magnify the law, and make it honourable.' God's judgements make known his glory as Isaiah 5:16 declares: 'But the LORD of hosts shall be exalted in judgement, and God that is holy shall be sanctified in righteousness.' The aim or design of Christ's death for our sins, according to Romans 3:26, is 'to declare, I say, at this time [God's] righteousness: that he might be just, and the justifier of him which believeth in Jesus'.

God's majesty is also seen in his love and mercy. 'There is forgiveness with thee, that thou mayest be feared' (Ps. 130:4). According to 1 John 4:10:

'Herein is love, not that we loved God, but that he loved us, and sent his Son to be the propitiation for our sins.' All of our future hope may be summarized by Revelation 22:4: 'And they shall see his face.' We will see the river of living water from which we will drink for ever, yes, and in which we shall bathe and immerse ourselves — this is the radiant vision of God shining in the face of Jesus Christ. As the first answer of the *Westminster Catechism* so wonderfully states: 'Man's chief end is to glorify God and to enjoy him for ever.'

The experiential and relational knowledge of God's glory is communicated to us in an experiential knowledge of sin, of Christ and his salvation, and our grateful obedience and worship. The *Heidelberg Catechism* (Q. 2) says,

How many things are necessary for thee to know, that thou, enjoying this comfort, mayest live and die happily? Answer: Three; the first, how great my sins and miseries are; the second, how I may be delivered from all my sins and miseries; the third, how I shall express my gratitude to God for such deliverance.

This threefold way of experiencing blessedness and comfort in Christ follows the pattern of experiential doctrine revealed in Paul's Epistle to the Romans, that part of the Bible above all others which God used to ignite the Reformation and the evangelical movement.

Experiencing the misery of sin

Romans 1:18 says, 'For the wrath of God is revealed from heaven against all ungodliness and unrighteousness of men, who hold the truth in unrighteousness.' The majestic God, maker of heaven and earth, has revealed his wrath, even hatred against sin (Ps. 5:4-6; 11:4-7). His holy revulsion burns against 'all ungodliness and unrighteousness', every bit of sin, every spot of spiritual dirt. This is not a doctrine to be quickly passed by on our way to more pleasant subjects. Paul devoted most of the first three chapters of Romans to an exposition of our rebellion against God and God's righteous anger against us. God's wrath against sin is 'revealed from heaven'. Think of the long history of the prophets' ministry, announcing and expounding Jehovah's 'controversy with the nations' (Jer. 25:31). God is 'willing to shew his wrath' (Rom. 9:22). The goodness and justice of God compel him to hate sin, to punish it, and to expunge it from his creation.

God's instrument to awaken us to the misery of sin is his holy law. Romans 3:20 tells us: 'by the law is the knowledge of sin'. God's law reveals the righteousness required of human beings, as creatures made in his image, and his sentence of condemnation upon all ungodliness and unrighteousness of sinful humanity. It does not do so in an abstract way, as an academic or philosophical discussion of metaphysics and ethics. God revealed the law in personal terms, as a word of command, given with 'the thunderings, and the lightnings, and the noise of the trumpet, and the mountain smoking' (Exod. 20:18). Who can live with a consuming fire (Heb. 12:29)? Who can dwell with everlasting burnings (Isa. 33:14)?

Even today the law of God presses into our consciences with burning words. The Scripture pierces beyond obvious sins to reveal the core of sin: our disdainful rejection of God and continual running after idols (Rom. 1:18-32). It turns our self-righteous judging of others against ourselves and says, 'You are the man' (*cf.* Rom. 2:1-4). It carries us to Judgement Day, to witness before God's throne the justice to come; the indignation, wrath, tribulation and anguish to fall on sinners, both those who have the law written in the Book and those who do not have the Book, but still have the law written on the heart (Rom. 2:5-16). No one will have any excuse, for all have sinned.

The law strips away our confidence in outward religious privileges and shows us that only a new heart ruled by the Holy Spirit will suffice (Rom.

2:17-29). It silences our complaints against God's justice and asserts his faithfulness and right to judge the world (Rom. 3:1-8). It puts us in the same place as all mankind under sin: no one is righteous, no one understands, no one seeks after God. Everyone is guilty before God, and nothing we do can make up for it (Rom. 3:9-20). Can we say we believe these fearsome truths if we do not feel them deeply?

The misery of sin is not merely a phase we pass through during our conversion. It is true that in one sense we can and should leave behind the misery of sin once we begin trusting in Christ. 'Being justified by faith, we have peace with God through our Lord Jesus Christ' (Rom. 5:1). The Spirit of Christ is the Spirit of adoption who quiets the horror of the conscience and the terror of divine wrath. At the same time our grief over sin increases with the closeness of our walk with God. So the evangelical Christian cries out: 'O wretched man that I am!' (Rom. 7:24), for he is the one who feels most keenly the war between the flesh and the Spirit.

Part of the poverty of the church today is that sin feels so light and can be dealt with so casually. We do not feel the weight of God's glory. All sin is enmity against God (Rom. 8:7). John Owen wrote: 'He that hath slight thoughts of sin had never great thoughts of God.'[60] How we need a renewed sense of the righteousness and majesty of God communicated to us through knowing the greatness of our sin and misery.

Experiencing the mercy of Christ

Romans 3:21-22 says, 'But now the righteousness of God without the law is manifested, being witnessed by the law and the prophets; even the righteousness of God which is by faith of Jesus Christ unto all and upon all them that believe: for there is no difference.' The righteous God did not jettison his righteousness in order to save sinners; he satisfied his righteousness through his Son, Jesus Christ. Christ is everything to the evangelical believer.

Paul spends the last verses of Romans 3 and the several chapters after it expounding the infinite riches of God's grace in Christ Jesus. These chapters are packed with doctrinal truth. Yet they also burn hot with vibrant evangelical experience. How foolish it would be on a cold day to sit by a fireplace stacked with seasoned wood and never start a fire! The teachings of Romans about the grace of Christ are solid logs of evangelical truth designed to burn bright and hot in our hearts. May the Spirit ignite them! Recall the encounter of John Wesley with Romans, as he wrote:

In the evening I went very unwillingly to a society in Aldersgate Street, where one was reading Luther's preface to the Epistle to the Romans. About a quarter before nine, while he was describing the change which God works in the heart through faith in Christ, I felt my heart strangely warmed. I felt I did trust in Christ, Christ alone, for salvation; and an assurance was given me that He had taken away my sins, even mine, and saved me from the law of sin and death.[61]

In the Epistle to the Romans we find fire for the soul, for it answers the greatest question of all: How can I, a sinner, stand righteous before a just and holy God? How can I escape the everlasting fires of hell? Paul's epistle tells us that we can find deliverance only through justification by faith in Christ alone, and not by our works (Rom. 3:21 – 4:25). The peace we gain with God through our Lord Jesus Christ changes everything: our foundation is grace, our future is glory, our tribulations are training, and our assurance is love poured into our hearts by the Holy Spirit and demonstrated beyond all doubt on the cross of Christ (Rom. 5:1-11). Evangelical Christianity is not merely about believing. It boasts not in our faith, but in our reconciliation with God through Jesus Christ.

The heart of Christian experience is union with Christ, grounded on his covenantal relation to us as our new, obedient Adam (Rom. 5:12-21) and worked out in our dying with Christ to sin, and rising with Christ to live to God (Rom. 6). Like a good sergeant training young recruits, Paul instructs us about our spiritual warfare against sin, describing how the battle will include struggles and frustrations (Rom. 7), but will ultimately result in victory by the Spirit of Christ (Rom. 8). God is working out his sovereign plan of salvation, and we may be assured that his promises will never fail. To him will be the glory for ever and ever (Rom. 9 - 11).

Paul erupts with praise in these Scriptures as he meditates on God's sovereign grace toward us in Christ. This is the complete answer to all our needs and a stunning display of God's glory (Rom. 8:28-39; 11:33-36). Nothing is more God-centred and Trinitarian than experiencing the truth and power of the gospel of sovereign grace. The *Heidelberg Catechism* (Q. 1) summarized that experience in words that have won a place in the heart of many evangelical Christians all over the world:

What is thy only comfort in life and death?

That I with body and soul, both in life and death, am not my own, but belong unto my faithful

Saviour Jesus Christ; who, with His precious blood, hath fully satisfied for all my sins, and delivered me from all the power of the devil; and so preserves me that without the will of my heavenly Father, not a hair can fall from my head; yea, that all things must be subservient to my salvation, and therefore, by His Holy Spirit, He also assured me of eternal life, and makes me sincerely willing and ready, henceforth, to live unto Him.

Experiencing the magnitude of gratitude

Romans 12:1-2 says, 'I beseech you therefore, brethren, by the mercies of God, that ye present your bodies a living sacrifice, holy, acceptable unto God, which is your reasonable service. And be not conformed to this world: but be ye transformed by the renewing of your mind, that ye may prove what is that good, and acceptable, and perfect, will of God.' Our response to God's mercy in Christ, then, is to devote ourselves to the daily doing of his will. There is nothing more satisfying for the redeemed than to give themselves to God, knowing that he 'spared not his own Son, but delivered him up for us all' (Rom. 8:32).

Wilhelmus á Brakel said the essence of religion is to live unto God at all times. He added: 'All that

God wills, the servant of God also wills, because the will of God is the object of his desire and delight.'[62] Cotton Mather wrote: 'If I may in any act of obedience, or of submission, to the will of God, be a grateful spectacle to him, or if he may take satisfaction in what he helps me to be, and to do, before him, this is the highest felicity I can wish for; the top of my ambition.'[63] Joyful submission to our covenant God is the hallmark of evangelical theology.

The evangelical Christian experience is not just an inner, private matter, but a practical doing of God's will in God's world. Christ's love for us moves us to humbly serve his church according to our spiritual gifts (Rom. 12:3-13), to bear patiently with enemies and overcome evil with good (Rom. 12:14-21), and to submit to the authorities that God ordained (Rom. 13:1-8). The grace of Christ motivates us to obey the Ten Commandments in the spirit of love (Rom. 13:9-10), to purify ourselves from worldliness and uncleanness in hope of Christ's coming (Rom. 13:11-14), and to live in meekness towards Christian brothers even when we disagree, so that we can worship God with one voice and great joy (Rom. 14:1 – 15:13). The gospel makes us, with Paul, strive by our prayers and personal witness for the spread of the gospel, so that the nations may be an acceptable offering to God, a great living sacrifice sanctified by the Holy Spirit (Rom. 15:14–33). This evangelical experience of gratitude flows out of Romans chapters twelve to fifteen. It is the living sacrifice of each redeemed individual culminating in the gathering in and purifying of all the elect from all nations as one great living sacrifice to the glory and pleasure of God.

This gratitude flows out of our hearts, Paul says, as we contemplate 'the mercies of God'. Evangelical obedience is gratitude in the deepest sense. It is love for God stirred up in us by his grace to us. He who has experienced much grace from God has much love for God. Isaac Watts captured it well in his hymn, 'When I Survey the Wondrous Cross':

> Were the whole realm of nature mine,
> That were a present far too small;
> Love so amazing, so divine,
> Demands my soul, my life, my all.

CONCLUSION

In summary, evangelicalism is gospel-driven Christianity, recognizable by the biblical fundamentals of the gospel of Christ, the Reformation fulness of the doctrines of Christ, and the practical fruit of the Spirit of Christ. Evangelicalism is not less than doctrine, but it is more than mere talk.

Some people only talk about their sin. They will freely tell you about how miserable, hopeless and sinful they are, but you do not see a broken heart and a contrite spirit in them. You do not see a love for Christ and desperate need for him. The marks of real evangelical experience are missing.

Other people talk a lot about Jesus. They believe in Jesus and him crucified. They know about his redemptive work. They talk about his grace and mercy, his willingness, and his power. But you never hear them talk about their genuine need for a Saviour. The fruits of their lives do not manifest humble gratitude. Their talk is a substitute for genuine experience. They talk about being on the Rock, but have never been in the horrible pit of knowing their sin. So they are slow to serve the Saviour.

Still others serve God in seemingly wonderful, admirable ways. They are busy and active people who have much to thank the Lord for in their prayers. They have much to do; they lend a helping hand to others and much of what they do puts others to shame. Yet you get the uncomfortable feeling that their talk and their walk are much like that of the Pharisee in Luke 18:11-12: 'God, I thank thee, that I am not as other men are, extortioners, unjust, adulterers, or even as this publican. I fast twice in the week, I give tithes of all that I possess.' You miss the humble gratitude of a true believer who abhors himself as a sinner, and repents in dust and ashes before a gracious Redeemer.

A truly evangelical experience contains a beautiful blend of historic gospel truths applied to one's life. What does it mean to experience true evangelicalism? By the Spirit's grace, *it is to know, feel and practically apply the majesty of God, the misery of sin, the mercy of Christ, and the magnitude of gratitude.* May God grant us all a more rich and continual experience of these things through his gospel.

NOTES

1. 'Notes' from the October 1888 *Sword and Trowel*, reprinted in *The 'Down Grade' Controversy* (Pasadena: Pilgrim Publications, 1978), 67.

2. Throughout this article I have refrained from capitalizing evangelicalism and evangelical to distinguish it from the amorphous entity that it is today.

3. Mark A. Noll, *Between Faith and Criticism: Evangelicals, Scholarship, and the Bible* (San Francisco: Harper and Row, 1986), 2.

4. *The New Cassell's German Dictionary* (New York: Funk & Wagnalls, 1971), 145.

5. David W. Bebbington, *Evangelicalism in Modern Britain: A History from the 1730s to the 1980s* (London: Unwin Hyman, 1989), 3.

6. John G. Stackhouse Jr, 'Defining "Evangelical"', *Church and Faith Trends* 1, no. 1 (2007): 3.

7. ISAE, 'Defining the Term in Contemporary Times', http://isae.wheaton.edu/defining-evangelicalism/defining-the-term-in-contemporary-times/ (accessed 13 April 2011). See Bebbington, *Evangelicalism in Modern Britain*, 2-3.

8. Richard Lovelace, 'A Call to Historic Roots and Continuity', in *The Orthodox Evangelicals*, eds Robert Webber and Donald Bloesch (Nashville: Thomas Nelson, 1978), 47. It should be noted that some of the participants in the 'Chicago Call' presented in this book left Evangelicalism to return to the Roman Catholic and Orthodox Churches.

9. *Cf.* W. Robert Godfrey, 'Martin Luther: An Evangelical Original', in *The Coming Evangelical Crisis*, ed. John H. Armstrong (Chicago: Moody Press, 1996), 45.

10. John H. Gerstner, 'Theological Boundaries: The Reformed Perspective', in *The Evangelicals*, eds David F. Wells and John D. Woodbridge, rev. ed. (Grand Rapids: Baker Book House, 1977), 25.

11. David Wells, 'On Being Evangelical: Some Theological Differences and Similarities', in *Evangelicalism: Comparative Studies of Popular Protestantism in North America, the British Isles, and Beyond, 1700–1990* (Oxford: Oxford University Press, 1994), 391-92.

12. NAE, 'What is an Evangelical?' http://www.nae.net/church-and-faith-partners/what-is-an-evangelical (accessed 13 April 2011).

13. NAE, 'Statement of Faith', http://www.nae.net/about-us/statement-of-faith (accessed 13 April 2011).

14. David Hilborn, 'Evangelicalism: A Brief Definition', http://www.eauk.org/about/what_is.cfm (accessed 13 April 2011).

15. Roger E. Olson, 'What is Evangelicalism?' http://rogereolson.com/2010/07/29/my-first-foray-into-blogging-what-is-evangelicalism/ (accessed 14 April

2011). Olson is a self-described 'postconservative' who desires to retain some connection to historic evangelicalism while rejecting its 'traditionalism'. He creates a dichotomy between experience and community on the one hand and doctrine on the other, and sees the former as the authentic heart of evangelicalism. *Cf.* Justin Taylor, 'An Introduction to Postconservative Evangelicalism and the Rest of this Book', in *Reclaiming the Center: Confronting Evangelical Accommodation in Postmodern Times*, eds Millard J. Erickson, Paul Kjoss Helseth, and Justin Taylor (Wheaton: Crossway Books, 2004), 17-21. For a critique of Olson's postconservativism, see R. Albert Mohler Jr, 'Reformist Evangelicalism: A Center without a Circumference', in *A Confessing Theology for Postmodern Times*, ed. Michael S. Horton (Wheaton: Crossway, 2000), 141-44.

On a related theme see also the recent collection of essays in *New Perspectives for Evangelical Theology: Engaging with God, Scripture and the World*, ed. Tom Greggs (London: Routledge, 2010). As Greggs lays out in the introductory essay, the group of 'younger scholars' in this book seek for an 'opening' of evangelicalism, arguing the 'rainbow-like' definition of evangelicalism finds itself in the movement 'towards a post-critical and formative theology' (1-13).

16. Roger E. Olson, 'Addendum to my first post about evangelicalism', http://rogereolson.com/2010/07/31/addendum-to-my-first-post-about-evangelicalism/ (accessed 14 April 2011).

17. James Montgomery Boice, preface to *Here We Stand! A Call from Confessing Evangelicals for a Modern*

Reformation, eds James Montgomery Boice and Benjamin E. Sasse (Phillipsburg, N.J.: P & R, 1996), 9.

18. Boice, preface to *Here We Stand!* 9-10.

19. D. G. Hart, *Deconstructing Evangelicalism: Conservative Protestantism in the Age of Billy Graham* (Grand Rapids: Baker, 2004), 32. *Cf.* Chad Owen Brand, 'Defining Evangelicalism', in *Reclaiming the Center*, 282.

20. Mohler, 'Reformist Evangelicalism', in *A Confessing Theology*, 146.

21. David Martyn Lloyd-Jones, *What Is an Evangelical?* (Edinburgh: Banner of Truth Trust, 1992), 18-25.

22. Lloyd-Jones, *What Is an Evangelical?*, 34-40.

23. Francis Turretin, *Institutes of Elenctic Theology*, trans. George Musgrave Giger, ed. James T. Dennison Jr (Phillipsburg, N.J.: P & R, 1992), 1:48-54.

24. John Calvin, *Institutes of the Christian Religion*, ed. John T. McNeill, trans. Ford Lewis Battles (Philadelphia: Westminster Press, 1960), 1025-26 [4.1.12].

25. *Heidelberg Catechism*, Q. 19.

26. 'The Gospel of Jesus Christ: An Evangelical Celebration', *Christianity Today* (14 June 1999): 51-56 (quotation from p. 52). Also available at: http://www.christianitytoday.com/ct/1999/june14/53.0.html (accessed 19 April 2011); *This We Believe*, eds John N. Akers, John H. Armstrong, and John D. Woodbridge (Grand Rapids: Zondervan, 2000), 239-48; J. I. Packer and Thomas C. Oden, *One Faith: The Evangelical Consensus* (Downers Grove, Ill.: InterVarsity Press, 2004), 185-95.

27. Lovelace, 'A Call to Historic Roots and Continuity', in *The Orthodox Evangelicals*, 45.

28. See Cameron A. MacKenzie, 'The Evangelical Character of Martin Luther's Faith', in *The Advent of Evangelicalism: Exploring Historical Continuities*, eds Michael A. G. Haykin and Kenneth J. Stewart (Nashville: B & H Academic, 2008), 171-98.

29. Bebbington, *Evangelicalism in Modern Britain,* 20.

30. Thus Oxford historian Diarmaid MacCulloch, rather than using the term 'Protestant' to describe the Reformers, prefers to use the term 'evangelical', writing: 'That word has the advantage that it was widely used and recognized at the time, and it also encapsulates what was most important to this collection of activists: the good news of the Gospel, in Latinized Greek, the *evangelium'*. Diarmaid MacCulloch, *The Reformation: A History* (New York: Viking, 2003), xviii.

31. Edwards saw himself as standing in an era 'which begins with the Reformation and reaches to the present time' during which God had greatly reduced the power of antichristian Rome by men like Luther and Calvin. See *The Works of Jonathan Edwards, Volume 9, A History of the Work of Redemption*, ed. John F. Wilson (New Haven: Yale University Press, 1989), 421-22. *Cf.* Douglas A. Sweeney and Brandon G. Withrow, 'Jonathan Edwards: Continuator or Pioneer?' in *The Advent of Evangelicalism*, 280-84.

32. Vernon Grounds, 'The Nature of Evangelicalism', *Eternity* (February 1956): 12-13.

33. Grounds, 'The Nature of Evangelicalism', 43.

34. For expositions of these Reformation principles, in addition to the major works of Luther, Calvin and the other Reformers, see Joel R. Beeke, *Living for the*

Glory of God: An Introduction to Calvinism (Lake Mary, Fl.: Reformation Trust, 2008); Sinclair B. Ferguson, *In Christ Alone: Living the Gospel-Centered Life* (Lake Mary, Fl.: Reformation Trust Pub., 2007); Terry L. Johnson, *The Case for Traditional Protestantism: The Solas of the Reformation* (Edinburgh: Banner of Truth Trust, 2004); Don Kistler, ed., *Sola Scriptura!: The Protestant Position on the Bible* (Morgan, Pa.: Soli Deo Gloria, 1995); John Piper, *Finally Alive: What Happens When We are Born Again* (Ross-shire, U.K.: Christian Focus Publications, 2009); Thomas R. Schreiner and Bruce A. Ware, eds, *Still Sovereign: Contemporary Perspectives on Election, Foreknowledge, and Grace* (Grand Rapids: Baker Books, 2000); R. C. Sproul, *Faith Alone: The Evangelical Doctrine of Justification* (Grand Rapids: Baker Books, 1995).

35. Lloyd-Jones, *What Is an Evangelical?* 44-51; Brand, 'Defining Evangelicalism', in *Reclaiming the Center*, 296-304.

36. Alliance of Confessing Evangelicals, 'The Cambridge Declaration', 20 April 1996, http://www.alliancenet. org/cc/article/0,,PTID307086_CHID798774_ CIID1411364,00.html (accessed 18 April 2011).

37. 'The Large [German] Catechism of Dr. Martin Luther', 4.57, in *The Book of Concord: The Confessions of the Evangelical Lutheran Church*, eds Robert Kolb and Timothy J. Wengert (Minneapolis: Fortress Press, 2000), 464.

38. Letter XXXVIII, 'To Mr. John Smith', 28 Sept. 1745, in *The Works of the Reverend John Wesley* (New York: J. Emory and B. Waugh, 1831), 6:623.

39. John Wesley, *Sermons on Several Occasions* (London:

Thomas Tegg, 1829), 1:vi.

40. 'The Cambridge Declaration', in *Here We Stand!* 14.

41. 'Evangelical Manifesto', 7, http://www.anevangelicalmanifesto.com/docs/Evangelical_Manifesto.pdf (accessed 13 April 2011).

42. 'Evangelical Manifesto', 8.

43. Joseph M. Stowell, 'The Evangelical Family: Its Blessings and Boundaries', in *This We Believe*, 218.

44. R. Albert Mohler Jr, '"Evangelical": What's in a Name?' in *The Coming Evangelical Crisis*, ed. John H. Armstrong (Chicago: Moody Press, 1996), 33.

45. See Benjamin B. Warfield, *The Plan of Salvation* (Grand Rapids: Eerdmans, 1942).

46. On the devastating implications for the Christian faith of the denial of divine foreknowledge, see Bruce A. Ware, 'Defining Evangelicalism's Borders Theologically: Is Open Theism Evangelical?' *Journal of the Evangelical Theological Society* 45, no. 2 (2002): 193-212.

47. See the *Belgic Confession* (art. 13, 16); *Heidelberg Catechism* (Q. 1, 26-28); *Formula of Concord* (art. 11); *Thirty-Nine Articles* (art. 17); *Westminster Confession* (2.1-2; 3.1); *Westminster Shorter Catechism* (Q. 7, 11, 20).

48. Mohler, '"Evangelical": What's in a Name?' in *The Coming Evangelical Crisis*, 40.

49. J. Gresham Machen, *Christianity & Liberalism* (1923; repr., Grand Rapids: Eerdmans, 1999).

50. Carl R. Trueman, *Christianity, Liberalism, and the New Evangelicalism: Lessons from J. Gresham Machen* (Bristol, Eng.: Onesimus Books, 2002), 11.

51. Wells, 'On Being Evangelical', in *Evangelicalism*, 399.

52. Kantzer, 'Unity and Diversity', in *The Evangelicals*, 75.

53. Robert Burns, introduction to the *Works of Thomas Halyburton* (London: Thomas Tegg, 1835), xiv–xv.

54. 'Epistle to the Reader', in *Westminster Confession of Faith* (Glasgow: Free Presbyterian Publications, 2003), 6.

55. Richard Niebuhr, *The Kingdom of God in America* (1937; repr. New York: Harper & Row, 1959), 193.

56. Niebuhr, *The Kingdom of God in America*, 192.

57. D. Martyn Lloyd-Jones, *Preaching and Preachers* (Grand Rapids: Zondervan, 1972), 98.

58. John Piper, *The Supremacy of God in Preaching*, rev. ed. (Grand Rapids: Baker Books, 2004), 24.

59. Quoted in John Stott, *Between Two Worlds: The Art of Preaching in the Twentieth Century* (Grand Rapids: Eerdmans, 1982), 31.

60. 'An Exposition upon Psalm 130', in *The Works of John Owen*, ed. William H. Goold (New York: Robert Carter & Brothers, 1851), 6:394.

61. 'Wednesday, May 24 [1738]', *The Journal of John Wesley* (Chicago: Moody Press, 1974), 64.

62. Wilhelmus á Brakel, *The Christian's Reasonable Service*, trans. Bartel Elshout, ed. Joel R. Beeke (Grand Rapids: Reformation Heritage Books, 1999), 1:4.

63. Cotton Mather, *Manuductio ad Ministerium: Directions for a Candidate of the Ministry* (1726; facsimile repr., New York: Columbia University, 1938), 10.

A wide range of Christian books is available from EP Books. Details of all our literature can be viewed online at our web site:

www.epbooks.org

EP BOOKS
Faverdale North
Darlington, DL3 0PH, England

e-mail: sales@epbooks.org